Rays of Light and Darkness

poems by

Raymond Turco

Finishing Line Press
Georgetown, Kentucky

Rays of Light and Darkness

To the Rutherford Red Wheelbarrow Poets

ACKNOWLEDGMENTS

I would like to thank the below journals for publishing some of the poems
featured in this chapbook:

The Rutherford Red Wheelbarrow ("Cosimina", "Alice degli spiriti", "Embers",
"My Grandfather's Voice")
The Lothlorien Poetry Journal ("Letters", "The Gods Who Rule the Earth",
"That Empty Jar", "The Shepherd of Many Turns", "The Ship of My Brothers")
Ovunque Siamo Press ("As a Blind Man Travels")

Publisher: Leah Huete de Maines
Editor: Christen Kincaid
Cover Art: Raymond Turco
Author Photo: Raymond Turco
Cover Design: Elizabeth Maines McCleavy

Order online: www.finishinglinepress.com
also available on amazon.com

Author inquiries and mail orders:
Finishing Line Press
PO Box 1626
Georgetown, Kentucky 40324
USA

Contents

I. From the Old World to the New

Spaesato

I no longer know where to bang my head.
I exist *ormai* between languages,
with each foot in a different country
I am alone, as they say, *spaesato*.

My brother-in-arms in this trench war of life
is Ungaretti Giuseppe, *poeta*,
who taught me the art of brevity
and what it means to be lost.

In Italy, I am American but different.
In America, I am Italian but quirky and new.
To belong this way and that
is to belong to no place,
the shame of my soul.
I am ever the stranger to myself,
it is my heart the most ruined country.

Cosimina

Cosimina reveled in the afterglow
of late-night parties between the wars,
and cozied up to her husband John
at the end of well-worn nights
punctuated by cigarette smoke
and chased down with spurts of poker games.

1941 was a vicious year for her,
the year of *refrigerator mother*
and a terrifying confusion
that winks at a nascent disease,
the ignominious one
that was often shuffled under carpets
or forever locked away in hospital
where no one could ever find out.

Misfortune split her mind in two,
a miscarriage of baby
and destiny.
A storm began to bellow inside her—
nice fellow John was,
to make coffee when she wasn't well,
bad smell
who can tell
it's all pell-mell,
she can hardly spell in her journal
which is by now frantic fits of fire
and rhapsody,
where roofs have pencil dark dirge demands
over a threatening sky skedaddled,
as the paranoia has met
the giddy and the giggling,
and all the ha-ha's when the neighbor died,
and the boo-hoos when daughter's on her period.
"Oh Christ John, what's happened to me?" she cried,
spied out of the corner of her eye, so sly,

a man walking outside who flim-flammed in such an
    extraordinary way
and begged to be attacked, so she ran out of the nubby apartment
half-nude and walloped the poor guy 'til she was sent away to the
    farm.

Antipsychotics didn't do much good,
the chasers to early insulin's shocks,
the visitors in her head were gone
but she was torbid and much befuddled,
so very sleepy and so poor in life and spirit.
Words continued to come to her wrong,
like unexpected guests to whom she would say
"Go on!" when really no one was at home.
The visions never had nice things to say in reply,
the apartment was a cacophony, a pig-sty, no lie,
good surprise the trees outside are all angry
relapsing on themselves, gobbly-wobbly and full of gum spurts.
Red faces in the mask, horrid pershings in black-pocked earth,
worthy of spleen and gustos of wind, laughing fangs all the time.
"But why won't they leave me alone?" she'd wail
and run to her room,
and leave John alone with his newspaper and cigarette
and black coffee.

Years passed,
and as Cosimina grew old,
her split mind slowed down
and those unexpected guests no longer came around.
Her eyes and ears quit on her so she rested sweetly on her
    dementia,
John was interred
but it all passed above her
and she spent her final decade in a home,
waiting for dinner above all things,
and when it was quiet and dinner was already consumed,

she'd pipe up with a burp and ask "When is dinner coming 'round?"

I think of Cosimina to this very day
and her long years
and her tough years
and her small early pleasures.
How John would
dance the waltz with her
to take her mind off flim-flams and nubby things,
the angry faces in the wall,
and I wonder if I may ever have the courage
to ask in a silent room,
"When is dinner coming 'round?"

The Family Curse

My grandmother stuck out her hand to me,
reached out across the years,
and placed in my palm
her disease.
It weighed a ton for me
just as hers weighed ten,
and she said,
speaking out across the years:
"My life will be your life,
that institution's cold and waxy walls
will be your walls,
you will go deaf and blind at the sight
and sound of so many malignant demons.
You will suffer, as I have suffered."

And I cried out, in my bipolar rage that stood
before her sixty-year schizophrenia,
which was a monolith to my growing effigy of pain.
The little demons of sight and sound came running in
on the heels of night to torment me with their black warped faces
and cackles like a hyena's verse.
The tree branches at nightfall turned to thorny fingernails of
     witches' hands.

Year after year, I sent them back,
I procured for myself a tin armor,
and I chased those demons far and away from the heels of the
     night.
I procured for myself some manufactured solace,
my friends were the salts of the lithium earth,
and I felt that I was happy.

I thought of my grandmother's unending suffering
and shook my head,
satisfied that it would not be my fate,
those institution's walls,
those insulin shocks,

those nights of scampering scores
of the scourge of Satan.
I inhabited a new society braced in Risperdal
and responsibility.
And my effigy to illness remained an effigy,
never became a monolith,
and it sits guarded by bastions
named Resolve
and Resistance.

But still I tip-toe about,
glancing over my left shoulder,
waiting for those bastions to crumble.

My Grandfather's Voice

On Sundays, I'd visit you
and you'd give me pound cake,
make me meatballs and overcooked macaroni
I'd scarf down with the appetite
of a playful, curious child
who delighted in making scalable mountains of trees.

You had a voice that was not a voice,
not a whisper,
a nothing with no good larynx
that launched into endless tales
of wild New Jersey streets
and of rumbles with your iron boxing hands.

You had a machine, an electric throat back,
so you were a robot to me
who expressed love in gentle-firm hugs
with mechanical arms,
arms that once carried ice from old ice trucks on Bergenline
when you were a child of eight years old as I was then.

"See you next Sunday" was tenuous hope
in a metal sound.

The Chef

I am chopping carrots,
you are dictating
in the bright light of our kitchen.

You give out orders firmly
like an officer,
and I am the private soldier.
Emulsify,
sauté,
and boil.
Your feminine side
is a secret to me.

Your mother, my aunt,
once told me
that you were different
when you were a little girl,
and she couldn't pin down
what made you harsh
like dandelion greens.
When you enter our home
with winter on your heels,
you rail and curse till your face goes red.
Cooking is your mastered solace,
the tai chi of the table,
your respite from the world.
When you chide me,
I am humbled.
I feel abandoned.

But when I go on my many ways
out and about,
and I come home to my room
down the hall from yours,
I find something I did not do:
my bed is ready-made,
sheets tucked in,

pillows aesthetically placed.
A simple lamp is burning,
and I know
that it could have only been you
who kept the flame alive
to call me home.

Das Walterlied

Born was he in Viernheim Hessen
in the year nineteenhundredtwentyseven,
cold in January and before the storm
well before the Krieg,
in Weimar in liberality,
but was not a young liberal he
in the year nineteenhundredfortythree,
raised his right arm high did he,
young in spirit pale of face
Hitler-Youthful full of grace
believer in the master race,
fought in battle barely-won
yearned for years before nineteenhundredfortyone,
kept his knife but buried quickly all his guns,
surrendered deliberate to the Americans,
to whom he sold contra-cigarettes
to escape the hounding Soviets—
then gone to sleepy Teaneck
where he married for the second time,
and where he took a second creed,
though at home for fun he played the Horst-Wessel-Lied
and cared for second's daughter—wasn't his,
and loved his second woman deeply, deeply second son
whom he put aged five in-lap behind the wheel,
who bumped the car going pace of snail,
but Walter merely sat and laughed,
no more raised right arm with Kraft,
but basked in joys of simple Jersey leisure,
photographing natural scenes for his pleasure,
savoring suburban America,
if only measure by measure.

He died blood-sick in nineteenhundredninety,
but before that he saw the triumphant fall
of the long-time-once-eternal Berlin Wall,
from his unhopeful-hopeful-home-hospice bed
full in spirit—short on hours,

never after leaving Germany
did he return to glimpse the cornflowers.

But with his final breath he whispered,
holding hands of second son and wife imploring,
"Bloom, bloom in the splendor of this happiness,
this strife,
this hard-won-joyful-come-once-only life."

II. Hearty Laughs and Heavy Sighs

The Gods Who Rule the Earth

Let us say a few words for our son in his trying time:
When he was young
he was already old.
When he was born,
we sang him the *El malei rachamim*
and we will sing it again
before he is done,
like a lullaby.
Every word he writes is erased,
canceled
from the face of this earth,
and from the face of the other earths that may be.
Every breath he takes cannot fill his lungs,
his fingertips are black with plague.

For we are the gods that govern the world,
and you must tremble.
We come in swiftly brokered tenuous peace,
like a golden thread intertwined in the hair of fate,
though even fate belongs to us,
and rests within our domain
that is very much like a feud, but eternal.

So tremble,
because we till the earth
and will always till the earth
until your teeth fall from your faces
and you regret
ever having been born.

Te Deum

Tedium on a Sunday stroll,
needle bits by the roadside
and trash rolling on deserted streets.
Tedium on a Sunday stroll,
the Hagia Sophia is now a mosque
in an Istanbul that's not Constantinople.
There's no more *oratorio*
in a cathedral no more my own,
so I am left by myself, to myself.
The Church has changed sides
and I am all alone
on a Sunday stroll.

That Empty Jar

In my cabinet there is
an empty jar of marmalade
that stands alone, unregarded.
I think I'll fill it with my hopes and dreams today:
that empty jar of marmalade,
receptacle of my youth on display.

Were it to shatter on the floor,
what would become then
of my hopes and dreams therein contained?
Would they scatter to the air and dissipate
or would they melt there on the tile
to stain my every waking moment,
a reminder of my youth laid bare?

I think I'll keep my jar hidden,
so only I can reach it
locked away,
and my hopes, my dreams,
I'll eat them
every day
so I won't have to bear
to see
my life exposed, my will untested,
my shame that pains me night and day.

Letters

I have written you one-thousand letters
and planted them between my aorta
and my best intentions.
Only when I am dead
will you remove from my heart the letters,
so full of "hope you're well"
and "sorry to bother".
But it's on these pages that passion's ink
has bled by now
through every bit of whitest square.

Youth Left Out in the Rain

Chalk scrapes on the blackish board and so
there are assessments and appraisals.
I am a marionette with a head of maggots—
folks want to see me dance over the flaming sun.
No more clubhouses for me:
I've got work and my skin is sandpaper.
My teeth rot from the cigars
I've smoked over busy proposals.

When will they give me my gold coin?
I don't know who that is in the mirror
and they ask me to come to church,
but the oil's burning and there's not much left
of time and my forehead aches to dry
all my youths I haven't kept under umbrellas.

Pseudobulbar and Jelly

Let the ha-ha's fly
as you boo-hoo-hoo
on the bus as if you read
a treatise by Foucault,
I say to me and myself.
I am more myself
than I ever was before.
But poor old Woody never seemed this funny,
a director and playwright with a stroke of genius.
I've had my own stroke,
though there was little wit to be had
and much wincing.
Not now though,
as I ha-ha-ha my way
to the haberdasher
to get my new head sewn in.

We're Getting Slightly Off Track

Are you hip to the hippodrome,
or do your horses race backwards
into the sunset?
Do you care for the hippopotamus
like he cares for you?
He only eats you
because he loves you too much.
And I'll never eat you
because I love you too little.

III. The Sea Depths, the Heights of Depravity

Embers

Embers rise and take their shape
of many faces:
fathers, mothers, lovers all
within the fire, around the fire.
They rise up and melt to smoke
that wafts up to join
Heaven's hearth.

Très louche

Slotted metal spoon in conal shape
balancing
cradling
lofty sugar cube.
Above: pure as pure
water
trickles down
diluting
anise drink,
to swig
and make me now forget to think.

Cloudy as the absinthe sky tonight
over New York harbor shining bright.
Dreams awake
in fractals-fairies far away
though seeming close at hand
delusions quake.
Wormwood has infected gut,
speech now is queer
since tongue is rot.
Dead-drunk and perhaps a little high
though high it seems
is mostly hyperbolic lie,
and I am left besotted.

No more green spells for me I hope,
I walk the night and faintly grope
the walls for kind support of me
to raise
my lowly life,
my heart of hearts
depraved.

Alice degli spiriti

You were a slim little sparrow in a black beret,
harboring a hefty malaise beside me,
as winter's icy nails rapped the windowpane
of that boutique hotel that hosted our one-night stand
that lasted one whole week.

You came from across the sea
to come see me in the metropolis,
it was the child of daily telephone calls
fecund in promises.

Your icy green nails clawed at Lucky Strikes,
one after one after one,
and the bed was full in a *ménage à trois*
with your beloved Valium.

I caressed your ashen thighs,
tolerated your cigarette kisses,
your fastidious second stomach
that left you frequently hungry,
but you became drugged
and spewed vitriol in Italian and French
and cried to go home.

One night you fell asleep in my arms
as we watched a film,
one night you told me
you had something to say but didn't know how.
I reflected and placed the week on a scale,
and replied, "Don't say it, ever."

I watched your pink fur coat go away,
go away to JFK, back to the land of *bolognese*,
and I touched my heart
and regretted that I made you
a ghost at noon.

The Ship of My Brothers

I was enveloped in a peace that I could not abide,
drifting across the seas in my ship of old oak,
when I spied a brigantine out of the corner of my eye
that was racing to the end of the starry black night.

It was the ship of the seven sisters,
with sailors all beturbaned,
dreaming
and crying out, senseless, to that wine-dark sky:
"Aldebaran!
Aldebaran!
Aldebaran!"
And they plunged into the depths of true wisdom
that only madmen can know,
as they sailed on the back of the bull
and went down, down,
foundering into the horizon below.

And I'd like to go with them,
but I can't go now,
because I have a meeting with a ram and a whale
before the sun rises in the east,
and shines upon my bow.

III. The *Belpaese* and Beyond

The Shepherd of Many Turns

The door to the night
braced in ignorance and sweat
guards my trade:
I tend to my sheep
and bellow and whoop
my apostate song.
When I die,
I will pass from man
to ewe
to plant
to ant
to dust
in that great psychosis of the soul.
And I am afraid.
Who is there to comfort me,
for I am alone amongst my flock
astride the silent mountains of Calabria?

And you see,
we are so very afraid these times.

My Florence

You, junkie of the broken teeth, ask me for a cigarette
and I'll etch my life's history
onto rolling paper
but I won't give it to you.
Each man should smoke his own destiny.

This was Florence to me:
vagrants pissing in Piazzale Michelangelo,
amateur philosophers postulating and pustulating
in Piazza della Signoria or outside the Red Garter, drunk
    again
and shoulder to shoulder with politicians
that pander to the populace
and pawn away
the energy of the whole town.
And I lived there in the blink of an eye,
enough to catch its hidden stench
that was divine inspiration
and Americans babbling over weed.

My autumn city,
once you were the gemstone of the peninsula,
so full of Dante and Lorenzo
that I could have willed myself happy—
and so be it!
Di doman non c'è certezza.

But tomorrow's here and gone,
your Comedy is over now.
The Arno is overflowing
with a turbid English
that spews from the mouths
of inebriated holidaymakers.

Two Dogs

Say *Quinsàn* and hold tight to the bone of your ancestors,
say *Àesa* and let the bone fall from your jaws.
The eternal struggle of town against town
beyond the civility of Verona's walls.

As a Blind Man Travels

The Western Wall is notes perfumed
with a love two thousand years wide.
I accidently brush hands pressed
with sweat and hope.

The bazaar of Marrakech
is leather and sour sumac.
The vendors' ululations are
my call to morning prayer.
Though I haggle with no one,
I am never alone.

As I'm carried away in a whoosh
of motors, the streets of Trastevere
hold me tight and smell of tripe.
A laundress with the voice of a toad
barks *romanesco* at a man
from Bangladesh who hawks roses:
They are both Rome to me.

I can feel the cobblestones sinking
and hear the lagoon erode the gondolas,
but my *bigoli in salsa* whisper
in reassurance: There will always be
a Venice in my memories.

The Prague Clock of the Old Town Square
sounds like the face of a friend
as it rings out the places of the stars.
The underground trains speed
toward prosperity, the intercom
voices are a confident polka.

The salesmen of Soviet berets
sing dirges; their nostalgia
is their currency and their deceit.

Prague is the city of the future
of the past.

Cities without sight are
Luna Parks for the mind.

A Note on the Poem "Two Dogs"

This poem is inspired by a provincial legend that draws on the feud between two small towns outside of the city of Verona. In the legend, a hungry dog from the town of Quinzano (*Quinsàn* in the Veronese dialect) meets a dog from the town of Avesa (*Àesa* in the Veronese dialect), who carries a bone in his mouth. The dog from Quinzano, eager to steal that bone, asks the dog from Avesa where he's from. The dog from Avesa drops the bone from his mouth when saying "Avesa" due to the open vowel sound of the town's name; comparatively, "Quinzano" has a more closed vowel sound. The dog from Quinzano then takes the bone and runs off. This legend is an adaptation of a fable by Aesop titled "The Fox and the Crow". In the center of the town of Quinzano, there is a recent statue depicting a dog with a bone in its mouth.

Raymond Turco is a poet and playwright born in Hackensack, NJ, USA. He writes poems in English and Italian and has a special affinity for European history, travel, surrealism, magical realism, and absurdism. He holds a Master of the Arts in Psychology, and studied in New York, and in Florence, Italy, where he focused on Italian history and literature. He sits on the Board of Directors of the Cliffside Park Arts Association (CPAA) in Cliffside Park, NJ, and is also the organization's Director of Poetry and Literature, as well as the host of the monthly Grantwood Poetry Reading Series. In 2010, he participated in a young playwrights' workshop program run by Young Playwrights Inc., founded by Stephen Sondheim, in New York, NY, in which he premiered a short commission as a staged reading. His play *The Vacuous Case of Mister Um* was the recipient of an honorable mention at the 2012 Blank Theatre's National Young Playwrights Festival in Hollywood, CA, where two other plays of his, *The Red Crow* and *The End*, were nominated as semi-finalists in that same year. In 2022, *The Vacuous Case of Mister Um* was given a staged reading as part of the CPAA's outdoor summer Festival in the Park, in Cliffside Park, NJ. The author of nine stageplays, he has published his poetry in the *Rutherford Red Wheelbarrow, Lothlorien Poetry Journal*, and with Bordighera Press, among others.